Kid Pick!

Title: _____

Author: _____

Picked by: _____

Why I love this book:

_____

_____

_____

_____

_____

CONSTELLATIONS

ABDO
Publishing Company

A Buddy Book **by Marcia Zappa**

Buddy BOOKS
The Universe

VISIT US AT
www.abdopublishing.com

Published by ABDO Publishing Company, 8000 West 78th Street, Edina, Minnesota 55439.

Printed in the United States of America, North Mankato, Minnesota.
102010
012011

 PRINTED ON RECYCLED PAPER

Coordinating Series Editor: Rochelle Baltzer
Contributing Editors: Megan M. Gunderson, BreAnn Rumsch, Sarah Tieck
Graphic Design: Maria Hosley
Cover Photograph: *Getty Images*: Image Work/amanaimagesRF.
Interior Photographs/Illustrations: *Getty Images*: Dorling Kindersley (pp. 23, 25), French School (p. 19), SSPL (pp. 9, 25); *iStockphoto*: ©iStockphoto.com/essxboy (p. 29), ©iStockphoto.com/ScantyNebula (p. 9), ©iStockphoto.com/TerrainScan (p. 27); *NASA* (p. 30); *Photo Researchers, Inc.*: Herman Heyn (p. 11), Larry Landolfi (p. 13), Gerard Lodriguss (p. 11), Babak Tafreshi (p. 5); *Shutterstock*: Baloncici (p. 28), djgis (p. 7), Igor Kovalchuk (p. 7), Sergey Mikhaylov (p. 21), Vlue (p. 15).

Library of Congress Cataloging-in-Publication Data

Zappa, Marcia, 1985-
 Constellations / Marcia Zappa.
   p. cm. -- (The universe)
 ISBN 978-1-61714-687-9
 1. Constellations--Juvenile literature. I. Title.
 QB802.Z37 2011
 523.8--dc22
                         2010031065

Table Of Contents

What Are Constellations?

At night, tiny lights dot the sky. These lights are stars. On a clear night, you can see thousands of stars.

Long ago, people noticed patterns in the stars. They named these patterns and used them to map the sky. These patterns are known as constellations.

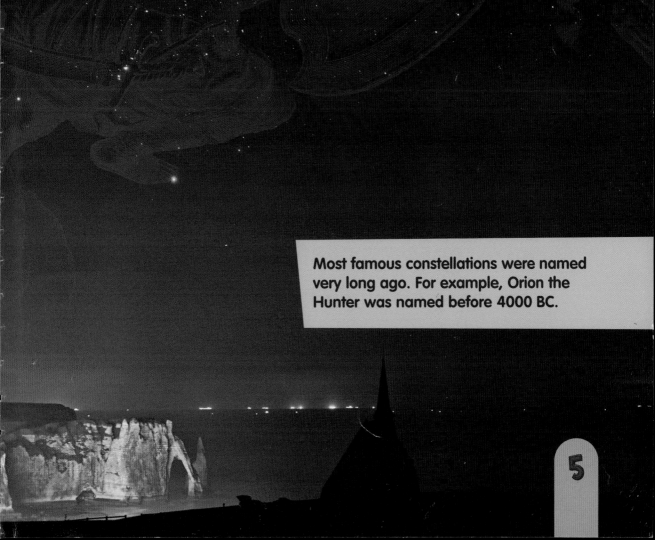

Most famous constellations were named very long ago. For example, Orion the Hunter was named before 4000 BC.

5

Starlight

Most stars are glowing balls of gas that give off light. There are many kinds of stars. They are different in size, **mass**, brightness, temperature, and color.

Stars are spread far apart across space. But from Earth, certain stars appear to be close together. These stars make up constellations.

Stars look small because they are far away. But, they are actually huge!

Our sun is the closest star to Earth. This makes it appear large and bright. The sun provides Earth with light and heat.

North or South

Not all constellations can be seen by everyone all the time. The ones you see depend on your location on Earth.

People near the North Pole see the constellations in the northern sky. People near the South Pole see the constellations in the southern sky. People near Earth's equator see the constellations in both skies.

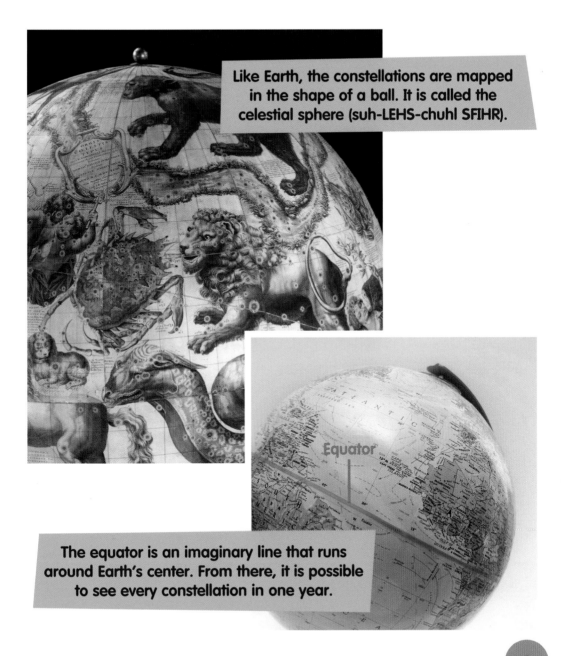

Like Earth, the constellations are mapped in the shape of a ball. It is called the celestial sphere (suh-LEHS-chuhl SFIHR).

The equator is an imaginary line that runs around Earth's center. From there, it is possible to see every constellation in one year.

Always Around

A few constellations can be seen year-round from certain places on Earth. These are called circumpolar constellations. They are located near either the North Pole or the South Pole.

Cassiopeia is a northern circumpolar constellation. It can be seen all year long by people on Earth's northern half.

The Southern Cross is a southern circumpolar constellation. It can be seen all year long by people on Earth's southern half.

Stars and Seasons

Many constellations can only be seen during certain seasons. These are called seasonal constellations.

It takes Earth one year to **orbit** the sun. As Earth changes position, seasons change. Different constellations can be seen.

That happens because our sun blocks the light of other stars. As Earth moves, stars behind the sun cannot be seen from Earth.

Your location on Earth affects when you see seasonal constellations. On Earth's northern half, Cygnus is a summer constellation. On Earth's southern half, it is seen in winter.

Move Along

Each night, constellations move across the sky. This happens because Earth is spinning.

As Earth **orbits** the sun, it spins on its **axis**. It takes one day for Earth to make a full spin. This action causes constellations to appear to cross the sky.

Constellations cross the
night sky from east to west.

15

Rise and Fall

Earth's **axis** is tilted. This causes different seasons. It also causes changing views of the night sky. As seasons change, circumpolar constellations appear higher or lower in the sky.

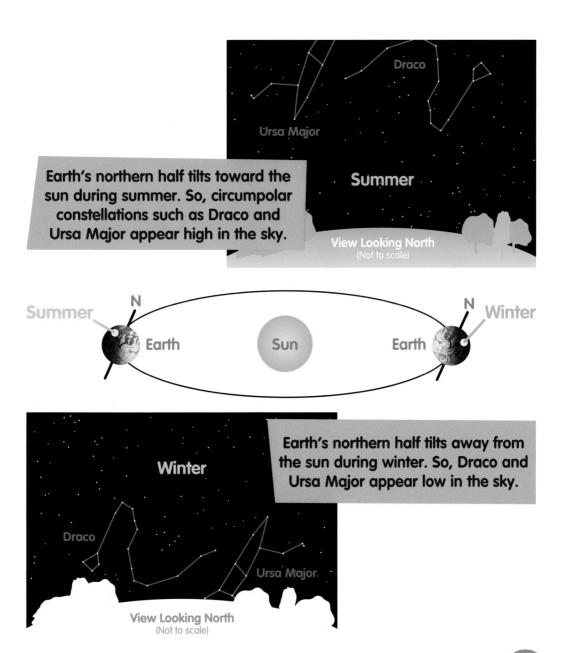

Draco

Ursa Major

Summer

View Looking North
(Not to scale)

Earth's northern half tilts toward the sun during summer. So, circumpolar constellations such as Draco and Ursa Major appear high in the sky.

Summer

N

Earth

Sun

Earth

N

Winter

Winter

Draco

Ursa Major

Earth's northern half tilts away from the sun during winter. So, Draco and Ursa Major appear low in the sky.

View Looking North
(Not to scale)

Early Constellations

People have been studying stars for more than 6,000 years. Long ago, poets, farmers, and scientists saw patterns in the night sky.

These patterns were useful to ancient people. They helped them locate certain stars. They were used to tell directions. And, they helped people track Earth's seasons.

Ancient sailors used constellations to direct their boats on the ocean.

Over time, star patterns in the sky became set constellations. They were named for animals, heroes, gods, and tools.

The constellation Hercules was named for an ancient Greek hero.

The constellation Leo was named for a lion.

Story Time

Many constellations were named for stories called myths. They often explained parts of life or nature that people didn't understand.

Long ago, people wondered what stars were. They wanted to know how they came to be in the sky. Many constellations are based on myths that explain this.

The Navajo tribe of Native Americans have a myth about a great bear. It explains how the stars in the constellation Ursa Major appeared in the sky.

Modern Meaning

In the beginning, ancient societies created their own constellations. Many of these patterns crossed over each other. And, stars were often in more than one constellation. This made it hard to keep track of them.

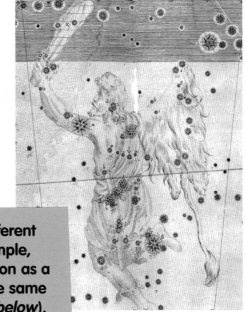

Ancient societies imagined different patterns in the stars. For example, Greeks saw the constellation Orion as a hunter (*right*). Egyptians saw the same constellation as the god Osiris (*below*).

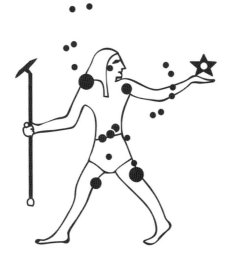

Scientists around the world saw a need for a more clear system. So in 1930, the International Astronomical Union (IAU) set 88 official constellations.

Today's constellations are based on ancient patterns. The IAU drew constellation borders so that every star was mapped. It also made sure that each star belonged to only one constellation.

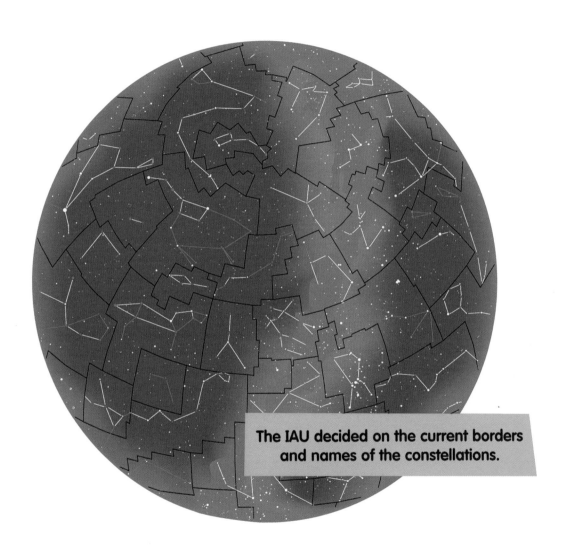

The IAU decided on the current borders and names of the constellations.

27

Fact Trek

Groups of related constellations are called families. Often, families appear close together in space.

The Zodiac is a famous constellation family. These 12 groups of stars form a line in space. They are popular fortune-telling tools.

Some of the best-known star patterns are only part of a constellation. They are called asterisms.

The Big Dipper is a well-known asterism. It forms a part of the great bear constellation Ursa Major.

Hydra is the largest constellation. It covers more than 3 percent of the sky. Hydra is known as the water snake constellation. It is long and thin.